Ballad. ~~with~~ ~~utterance~~ v.int. To make or sing ballads. Shak.

Ballader. n. A writer of ballads. ~~Scribbury.~~

~~Ballad-singer. n. One whose employment is to sing ballads.~~

Either from Heb. & Ch. □ ⅃ to weigh exactly, bring to a balance, or from

Ballast. n. [Sax. bat, a boat, D. boot & D. last, load, burden, G. last = Fr. lest lading; ballast. W. lluyth; Arm. lastr. ballast. Bat lost, boat lading, ~~corrupted~~ changed into ballast. ~~See boat.~~] Mar. ballast.

Heavy matter, as stone, sand, or iron, ~~and~~ laid on the bottom of a ship or other vessel, to sink it in the water, to such a depth, as to enable it to carry a sufficient sail, without oversetting.

2. Figuratively, that which is used to make a thing steady. Swift.

Ballast. v.t. To place heavy substance at the bottom of a ship or vessel, to keep it from oversetting.

2. To keep any thing steady, by counterbalancing its force. Dryden.

Ballasted. pp. Furnished with ballast; kept steady by a counterpoising force.

Ballasting. ppr. Furnishing with ballast; keeping steady.

Ballasting. n. Ballast; that which is used for ballast. Shak.

Shingle-ballast, is ballast of ~~coarse~~ coarse gravel.

Ballatoon. n. A heavy luggage boat employed on the rivers about the Caspian Lake. Mar. Dict.

ballet. It. baletto.

Ballet. n. [Fr. See ball, a dance.] A kind of dance; an interlude; ~~or~~ ~~dance in which some history is represented, or~~ ~~labour~~ a comic dance consisting of a series of several airs, with different movements, representing some subject or action. Encyc.

2. A kind of ~~poem~~ dramatic poem, representing some fabulous action or subject, in which several persons appear & recite things under the name of some deity or personage. Encyc.

Balliage or more correctly bailiage. n. [Fr. baile, a town. ~~balliage~~] A small duty paid ~~by~~ to the city of London by aliens, & even by denizens, for certain commodities exported by them. Encyc.

Noah Webster
WEAVER OF WORDS

Pegi Deitz Shea
Illustrated by Monica Vachula

CALKINS CREEK

Honesdale, Pennsylvania

With *amore*, to Brian Scanlon and Cathy Jannarone, who share the wonder of words
P.D.S.

To my husband, and to my mother
M.V.

Acknowledgments
  Thank you to Susan Bivin Aller, biographer
extraordinaire; to the "Wednesday Writers" for enduring
my drafts and helping me make Noah likable to young
readers.
  My gratitude goes to Christopher Dobbs, executive
director of the Noah Webster House and West Hartford
Historical Society, for a personal tour of the museum and
for his patience with all my e-mails, calls, and drafts.
  Thank you also to John Morse, president of
Merriam-Webster, for his tour, resources, and insight
into Noah Webster.
  Lastly, thank you to Carolyn P. Yoder, editor and
author, who pushed me to excel. No matter what I write,
I will always remember her question,
  "Where's the poetry?" —*P.D.S.*

Calkins Creek
An Imprint of Boyds Mills Press, Inc.
815 Church Street
Honesdale, Pennsylvania 18431
Printed in the United States of America

Cover and interior design by CPorter Designs

Library of Congress Cataloging-in-Publication Data

Shea, Pegi Deitz.
 Noah Webster : weaver of words / by Pegi Deitz Shea ;
illustrated by Monica Vachula. — 1st ed.
  p. cm.
 Includes bibliographical references and index.
 ISBN 978-1-59078-441-9 (hardcover : alk. paper)
 1. Webster, Noah, 1758–1843—Juvenile literature.
2. Lexicographers—United States—Biography—Juvenile
literature. 3. Educators—United States—Biography—
Juvenile literature. I. Vachula, Monica, ill. II. Title.

PE64.W5S45 2009
423.092—dc22
[B]

2009007312

First edition
The text of this book is set in 11–point Linoletter Medium.
The paintings are done in oil on board.

10 9 8 7 6 5 4 3

Page 21: Image courtesy of the Noah Webster House and
West Hartford Historical Society.
Endsheets: A page of an original manuscript, c. 1825, in
Noah Webster's hand, defining *B* words for *An American
Dictionary of the English Language*. By courtesy of
Merriam-Webster Inc. (www.Merriam-Webster.com), 2009.

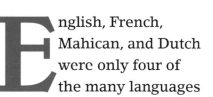

"HOW ARE YOU?"
"COMMENT ALLEZ-VOUS?"
"QUIN'A MONTH'EE?"
"HOE IS HET?"

English, French, Mahican, and Dutch were only four of the many languages spoken along the Hudson River during the time of the American Revolution. After America won its independence from Great Britain, people wondered, how can we create one nation when we can't even understand each other?

A patriot and scholar named Noah Webster suggested we unite through words. "A *national language* is a band of *national union* . . . for if we do not respect *ourselves* . . . *other nations* will not respect us."

Noah—whose last name means "weaver" in Middle English—wove words to unite the peoples of America.

Noah Webster is best known for writing American dictionaries. But that's not all he did. The man had the energy of a thousand bees, and knowledge was his nectar. He became America's first best-selling author. He published America's first spelling and reading texts, in addition to texts about American history and geography. He penned pamphlets against slavery. He wrote about politics, agriculture, and disease. Noah helped create the laws for the country's free public education system. His political writings and speeches helped form and pass the U.S. Constitution.

Noah Webster was a mighty patriot with a pen.

YOUNG THINKER

"I began life . . . full of confidence in my own opinions. . . ."

Noah Webster, Jr., was born on October 16, 1758, into a family that loved learning and believed in serving the public. Ancestors on both his mother's and father's side were governors. His father, Noah, a farmer and weaver, also served as a deacon and a justice of the peace. Noah's mother, Mercy, taught her son how to read, count, and play the flute.

The five Webster children—Mercy, Abram, Jerusha, Noah, and Charles—grew up in a clapboard house in the west division of Hartford, Connecticut. A huge center chimney opened to fireplaces in three rooms: the kitchen-dining room, an upstairs bedroom, and the parlor-bedroom, where Noah was born.

Noah's bushy red hair made him easy to spot as he helped harvest corn, flax, and hay on the ninety-acre farm. His strong, wiry build was perfect for digging potatoes, shearing sheep, and making flax into thread.

Noah liked tooting on his flute and reading much more than he liked reaping crops. He later confessed to his granddaughter that he would "take his Latin Grammar into the field" and that his "rests under the apple trees were quite too long for a farmer's son."

Noah's family had a history of government service. One of Mercy's ancestors, William Bradford, stepped off the *Mayflower* in 1620 and served off and on as governor of Plymouth, Massachusetts, for the next thirty years. Noah's father descended from John Webster, governor of Connecticut from 1656 to 1657.

"Amusing myself with books and with a flute" put some fun into Noah's farming days. He marveled at how "the sound of a little hollow tube of wood" took away "the heaviest cares of life!"

After a hard day's work, the Websters enjoyed music and literature. With a whale-oil lamp flickering on the long dinner table, the family read from the King James Bible. By fireside, they recited poetry, told stories, and sang psalms. These nightly performances prepared Noah to become a famous public speaker. He was hardly shy, and he appeared confident with his high forehead and jutting chin.

5

In the mid-1770s, not all the colonies provided "common," or public, schools for children. By state laws, Massachusetts and Connecticut towns had to set up schools *only* if they had at least fifty households. If settlers lived several miles away or in

6

rural areas, they had to fend for themselves. Children, needed for farm work in the warm months, went to school only in the winter.

Common schools existed in different settings. Noah attended a little schoolhouse—a two-mile trudge from his home. Puritan Congregational churches and public meeting houses usually offered space. Educated women held "Dame Schools" in their own homes. Teachers did not need a college degree. In colonial times, anyone who could read could teach.

Noah recalled the dismal conditions of the typical schoolroom, heated only by a lone stove. The teacher and students had few supplies. They used goose-quill pens and home-made ink from mashed nutshells, vinegar, and soot. "No geography was studied . . . no history was read . . . no book for reading was used," he said. "The teacher wrote the copies & gave the sums in Arithmetic; few or none of the pupils having any books as a guide." To practice spelling and penmanship, students copied Bible passages as the teacher dictated them.

Watching hay grow excited Noah more than attending common school. The students spent only one hour on studies, he said, "while five hours . . . was spent in idleness, in cutting tables and benches to pieces [for firewood, most likely], in carrying on pin lotteries, or perhaps in some roguish tricks."

In Webster's time, popular books written in English included *Robinson Crusoe* by Daniel Defoe, *Gulliver's Travels* by Jonathan Swift, *The Pilgrim's Progress* by John Bunyan, and *Utopia* by Sir Thomas More as well as plays and poems by William Shakespeare. Colonial readers found American essays, articles, plays, and poetry in weekly newspapers published in large cities. People also wrote political and religious pamphlets. One popular English author of psalms, hymns, and religious children's stories was Isaac Watts.

CONSTANT LEARNER

Noah sought knowledge the way a sail seeks wind. At fourteen, he wanted to study one-on-one with Hartford's new minister, Reverend Nathan Perkins. This Yale College graduate knew Latin and Greek, so Noah could learn to read ancient writings. Mr. Webster first said it cost too much. Noah kept begging and soon won out. In return, his father told him, "I wish to have you serve your generation and do good in the world and be useful."

After only two years, Rev. Perkins encouraged Noah to go to Yale. Again, Noah's father could not afford it. Yet, he mortgaged his house to get the money. Noah began studying at Yale in 1774. His proud father often rode the fifty miles to New Haven to visit Noah or to fetch him for holidays. At home, he'd find his siblings busy with the farm. His older brother, Abram, and his younger one, Charles, were also drilling with their father in the Hartford militia. Revolts against British laws and taxes and skirmishes with British soldiers were mounting.

If Noah had expected to leave his hard work back on the farm, he would have guessed wrong. Noah and his classmates called their dormitory the Brick Prison. Students had to split their own wood, build their own fires, and pump their own water. They rose at 5:30 a.m., prayed, then listened to lectures until their 9:00 breakfast. Common food at noontime was cornmeal mash called Injun Pudding or a soup made of cabbage, turnips, potatoes,

and dandelion greens. The boys actually liked their plain dinner of brown bread and milk better than anything else.

The students' day was filled with *ten* hours of instruction. Noah especially liked the advanced sciences. He studied plant

stems in botany class and stars in astronomy class. He fit in calculus and physics, along with philosophy and theology. He learned biblical languages such as Syriac, Hebrew, and Chaldee. Noah was weaving himself a coat of many colorful subjects.

Yale College, founded in 1701, is the third-oldest college in America. (Harvard College in Massachusetts was founded in 1636; The College of William & Mary in Virginia was founded in 1693.) Yale's students, for centuries all boys, ranged in age from twelve into their twenties. They came from important—but not necessarily wealthy—families who led the colonies in business, government, and the church. Most students hoped to become religious or political leaders.

In 1775, America's quest for independence from Great Britain became war. Younger Yale students such as Noah didn't have to fight. However, they argued plenty among themselves.

Noah didn't believe in "all work and no play." He made many friends at Yale and made quite a bit of mischief, too: laughing during chapel service, flirting with the ladies in town, throwing food at faculty, and using profane language. But he and his friends straightened out into "Yale's most distinguished class up to the Civil War." Noah's schoolmates included Oliver Wolcott, Jr., the future secretary of the treasury and later governor of Connecticut; Josiah Meigs, a Yale professor who became president of the University of Georgia; Zephaniah Swift, who became chief justice of the Connecticut Supreme Court; and Joel Barlow, a popular poet who became a diplomat in Europe. Throughout his life, Noah remained close with Timothy Dwight, who had worked as a tutor at Yale. An author and Calvinist minister, Dwight went on to become president of Yale in 1795. And Nathan Hale, a recent graduate, gave his life for independence. The British hanged him as a spy in September 1776.

The Loyalists, or Tories, wanted to stay tied to Great Britain. Patriots, like Noah, wanted no ties at all.

The Yale patriots formed a military company, conducted combat drills, and built barricades to protect New Haven, an important seaport between New York and Newport, Rhode Island. When marching,

Noah paced the soldiers with his flute music. Once, General George Washington and Major General Charles Lee were lodging in New Haven on their way to Boston. They asked the Yale regiment to escort their troops north out of town. Noah led the way, playing "Yankee Doodle" on his flute. Washington and Lee "expressed their surprise & gratification" at the students' precision.

The war caused hard times for everyone. Men had to fight, so they couldn't run their farms. That produced a shortage of food for humans and necessary animals such as cows and horses. The men couldn't run their shops, either. Important goods such as footwear, clothing, blankets, and weapons became scarce. Battles and port blockades prevented trading. Even if goods did make it inland, wives had little money to buy them.

Yale's faculty and students suffered, too. If young men were fighting, that meant there was less tuition money to help run the school. The colonists' paper money had become useless, anyway. One Yale dormitory building actually collapsed. Food ran out. Firewood dwindled to the point where students had to burn straw and cornstalks. Several times, Yale sent the students home. More boys then enlisted as soldiers—some for the English and some for the colonists.

WILLING SOLDIER

Noah joined his brothers, Charles and Abram, in their father's Hartford militia. "I marched, a volunteer, to the bank of the Hudson, ill able to bear the fatigues of a soldier & glad at times to find a bed of straw in a barn or shed."

The mission: trap British general John Burgoyne's troops, who had overtaken upstate New York. Noah's regiment camped across from Kingston. They had to prevent Burgoyne from meeting an English fleet sailing up from New York City. But Burgoyne never reached them. Near Albany, other militias had pushed Burgoyne's troops back north to Saratoga, where he surrendered. In revenge, the English fleet burned down Kingston, then fled south. The Hartford militia could do nothing but watch in horror from the east bank.

TEACHER AND LAWYER

Noah eventually returned to Yale and graduated in September 1778 at the age of nineteen. He was eager to follow his father's advice to "do good in the world and be useful." However, he soon suffered "extreme depression and gloomy forebodings." Jobs barely existed during wartime for a young, highly educated man. Some of his Yale friends were going to the Litchfield Law School in western Connecticut—the first one established in America. But Noah's family didn't have any money; and teaching in Hartford paid him too little to afford tuition. However, Noah did notice that the emerging leaders of the new nation were lawyers. So, in his spare time, he first studied law with a future U.S. Supreme Court justice, Oliver Ellsworth. He then apprenticed with Jedediah Strong, learning

the more common workings of the law, such as land deeds and business contracts. On top of these demands, Noah taught himself the French, German, Italian, and Spanish languages. He aimed to earn a master's degree in arts from Yale.

The year 1781 saw many triumphs for Noah Webster and the thirteen colonies. On March 1, the Continental Congress ratified the Articles of Confederation and named the colonies "The United States." On April 3, having passed his law exams, Noah was admitted to the Connecticut bar. On June 1 in Sharon, Connecticut, he opened a private, innovative school, which drew students also from New Jersey and New York. And in September, Noah earned his master's from Yale by writing a dissertation about how to improve public education.

In Noah's time, few books, essays, or poems were translated into English. So the more languages Noah learned, the more world literature he could read. He enjoyed Homer's *The Iliad* and *The Odyssey* in Greek, Miguel de Cervantes's *Don Quixote* in Spanish, and the philosophy of René Descartes in French. His favorite scholar was the mathematician, scientist, and philosopher Sir Isaac Newton, whose *Principia Mathematica* needed no translation from the English.

All these achievements, however, did not immediately add up to a comfortable living for Noah. Soldiers were still warring. Most men who had made it home in one piece could not afford a lawyer to solve problems such as arguments about land. So Noah continued teaching. He also earned a bit more money by writing essays for newspapers such as the weekly *Connecticut Courant* and the Boston area's *Salem Gazette*.

Noah's writings often attacked the shoddy shape of schooling. Noah loved teaching

books! Written by *American* writers!

American education needed reform, Noah wrote. Children should learn in small class sizes, "never more than twenty or twenty-five pupils under the charge of one instructor." Concerned about the students' health, Noah proposed better heating and comfortable chairs and desks. Teachers should reward good students instead of beating the troubling ones. Children wouldn't learn well "under the lash of a master's rod." Girls may learn dance and needlework at home, but they should also attend school to learn math, science, geography—the same subjects boys studied. Noah stated that adults should be able to attend school. Every citizen should be able to read, even slaves. (He argued against slavery, too.)

He wrote, "In our American republics, where government is in the hands of the people, knowledge should be universally diffused by means of public schools."

Noah saw firsthand the need for better and more uniform education for all citizens. While traveling to a new teaching job in Goshen, New York, Noah met idle soldiers and farmhands. Their words came from all kinds of European and Native American languages. And the people who could speak English had all sorts of accents. Even though Noah knew many languages, he could barely understand a word. Watching arguments erupt from misunderstandings, he felt powerless.

Then he got an idea about how to weave a stronger bond among American people: "Let us . . . establish a *national language* as well as a national government."

Noah, who admitted he was "vain" and "bold," decided to teach the whole country how to read, speak, and write American.

children and wanted to improve their education. However, it was hard without books and supplies for the students. Worse, instructors' books were all about England. He wanted to "engage children to be diligent and make them fond of books." New *American*

WORDSMITH

The teacher had several reasons to try reform. Noah thought that rich English people had made their spellings and pronunciations too fancy in order to separate themselves from the lower class. In fact, English dictionaries did not include the speech of commoners. Noah believed that Americans could and should use their own language to break free totally from England.

Noah got right to work on a "federal language." First, he studied the spellers written by English scholars Thomas Dilworth and Daniel Fenning. He wanted to improve upon their weaknesses. For example, both spellers asked children to memorize words with many letters and syllables before they had learned short words of one syllable. Some long words included biblical and British names and places. Of Dilworth's speller—the one Noah grew up using—he said, "One half of the work is totally useless, and the other half defective and erroneous."

Noah wanted words to be spelled the way they were pronounced in everyday usage and with the fewest letters as possible. That way, children could learn and remember the words' spellings more easily. Noah tried removing silent letters, making *bread* "bred," *give* "giv." He substituted a sound for words that didn't have a clear sound: *laugh* "laf," *mean* "meen," *blood* "blud." Most of Noah's spellings did not take hold. But some did: *plough* became "plow," *musick* became "music," *colour* became "color."

Noah wanted all Americans to pronounce

Noah learned during his speaking tours, beginning in 1782, that he could not change people's regional accents. And some people—many of them schoolmasters—resisted his spelling and pronunciation reforms. One religious newspaper reported, "Why, he's changing the psalms of David and making children say *salvashun* instead of *sal-va-ci-on*, the way we sing it in church."

words the same way, too. Dilworth had often broken words into syllables that did not follow the rules of English pronunciation,

for instance, "clu-ster" (cloo-ster) instead of "clus-ter." Noah's spelling book broke words into syllables that captured the way most colonists pronounced the words. For example, the British pronounced the suffix *ion* as two syllables, "ee-un." Webster noticed that most Americans had substituted the sound "un." For example, *action* is pronounced "ak-shun." He also corrected wrong spellings and pronunciations: not "chimbley," but *chimney*.

19

Perhaps most important, Noah created new ways to *teach* spelling, reading, and pronunciation. His book tried to make grammar fun and easy to learn. Dilworth grouped words together by how many letters they had: *babe, beef, best, bold*. Knowing how children loved rhymes, Noah made lists of words that sounded alike: *bog, dog, fog, hog, jog, log*. Later versions of his books even had illustrations. Noah made up rules teachers could share with students. For example, "The consonant *c* is hard like *k* before *a, o, u, l, r* . . . such as *cat, cord, cup* . . . but is always soft like *s* before *e, i, y*; as *cellar, civil, cypress*."

His speller also had a section for reading, which would become its own book in future printings. Noah wrote, "America must be as independent in *literature* as she is in *politics*, as famous for *arts* as for *arms*." Calling for "cultural independence," he published selections from Americans: Benjamin Franklin's proverbs, John Hancock's political essays, George Washington's speeches, Joel Barlow's and Timothy Dwight's poetry. The authors shared pages with England's William Shakespeare and Greece's Plato. Noah also included a letter denouncing slavery. Although this literature was already available to educated adults, Noah's speller was the first to make it accessible to beginning readers of any age.

The reading section didn't stop at language arts. "Every child in America should be acquainted with his own country," Noah believed. He became the first to publish American history and geography in children's textbooks. He listed important dates and events and the names of *American* towns, cities, counties, and states and their capitals in his readers. He included sections of the Declaration of Independence. The speller had almost every subject but math—which didn't need Americanization.

Noah's book went by several names in its history. His drafts were titled "The American Instructor." His first published title was a mouthful: *A Grammatical Institute of the English Language*. The 1788 edition took the name *The American Spelling Book*. Much later, when Noah was writing for advanced students, he called his original work "The Elementary Book." However, after the book's first appearance, readers fondly nicknamed it the "Blue-Backed Speller" or "Old Blue-Back" because of its blue binding. Over forty years, more than seventy million copies of the Blue Back would sell. At one time, there were more Blue Backs sold in the United States than Bibles.

Noah spent a good deal of his own money to print his books. He had to pay the publishers of the *Connecticut Courant* newspaper to print his first book. In turn the publishers sold it for ten cents unbound, sixteen cents when bound in sturdy blue paper. Five thousand copies sold out in nine months! Noah earned only a penny a book. By 1804, when the American population was only six million, 1.5 million Blue Backs had sold. But thousands were printed and sold without Noah's permission, and he did not receive a cent.

During his travels to promote copyright laws and his book, Noah shared his educational and political ideas with important American leaders. In particular, he spent much time with Benjamin Franklin. As early as 1749, Franklin had been promoting universal public education. Franklin wanted language reform, too. In fact, he'd already written down his own, more revolutionary ideas on spelling and pronunciation. Franklin had wanted a new alphabet, taking away the letters *c, w, y,* and *j,* and adding new letters and compound letters such as *ng.* Although Webster didn't agree on all reforms, Franklin became a great friend and mentor.

Once Noah had his educational ideas and methods published as a book, he could have it reprinted and sold to make money. But once others had the book, nothing stopped them from copying it and selling it, too.

In August 1782, Noah traveled to Philadelphia, where leaders of the Continental Congress were making new American laws. Noah persuaded them that people shouldn't be able to copy and sell someone else's work. Lawmakers, including future presidents Thomas Jefferson and James Madison, liked Noah's idea. But at this time, they recommended that the states handle copyright law themselves. It then fell to Noah to persuade each of the states' leaders. Friends such as Timothy Dwight helped Noah achieve copyright laws in New York, Massachusetts, and Connecticut. George Washington and Madison helped him succeed in Virginia.

Noah then traveled around the country, trying to set up copyright laws. In states that did not enact the laws, Noah negotiated directly with printers. They could publish and sell his speller for ten years, giving Noah a "royalty" of one cent per copy or a flat fee at the beginning. Either way, the money wasn't much; Noah took what he could get. He sincerely wanted his speller in everybody's hands so a national language would grow. Finally, Congress passed the Copyright Act of 1790, which Noah helped amend for more protection throughout his life.

POLITICAL AUTHOR AND SPEAKER

Noah's ideas about education depended upon a government of the people. He came to these beliefs by studying world history. "It is the business of *Americans* to select the wisdom of all nations as the basis of her constitutions, [and] to avoid their errours."

Noah wanted a hand in crafting the Constitution of the United States. In his book of four essays called *Sketches of American Policy* (1785), he called for a strong central government that protects its people and their property. This philosophy is called

Federalism. Noah likened this kind of government to the solar system, wherein the sun controls the planets, which in turn control the moons. He described how an elected congress can represent the states and make laws. He also wrote to abolish slavery and to separate the church and state.

Among the many notable political leaders who applauded Noah's writings were George Washington and James Madison. Washington congratulated Noah on *Sketches* and recommended passages for national publication and debate.

He also asked Noah to tutor his children and be his full-time secretary. But Noah responded, "I must write—it is a happiness I cannot sacrifice." A few years later, Madison quoted *Sketches* in his notes at the Constitutional Convention of 1787 and later wrote to Noah Webster, crediting him with several ideas that helped form the Constitution.

Noah had hoped to become Connecticut's representative at the Constitutional Convention. However, his articles about how to fund the new government made him controversial. Citizens rioted over whether the federal government or the states should make their own money and tax their own people, and whether funding should come from new paper money or taxes. Noah argued for a central federal government to tax the people. He called new paper money as worthless as "old horses." He infuriated New Englanders by writing that they were not yet educated highly enough to make such decisions. Not only did Noah lose the chance to represent Connecticut, but he also lost a lecturer position at the University of Pennsylvania. He also made an enemy of Thomas Jefferson, who championed the rights of individuals and states over the power of a central government. Noah Webster, Sr., advised his son "to be wise as a Serpent as well as harmless as a dove."

Noah still wanted to help form the country. After the Constitution was drafted, Noah wrote essays and gave speeches urging states to adopt the Constitution. On these trips, he also sold his books and made deals with printers. He was becoming popular, invited by government and society leaders to dinners and dances. His diary of October 1787, when he was editing the *American Magazine* in New York City, shows a mix of work and play.

During a visit in Philadelphia earlier that year, Noah met Rebecca Greenleaf. The twenty-one-year-old brunette, petite and graceful, soon joined Noah on his social engagements. When they were apart, he wrote often to "the lovely Becca," whom he found "witty, sensible, sociable." Once, he enclosed a keepsake: a lock of his red hair.

At first, Rebecca's wealthy parents did not approve of Noah because he didn't have a lot of money. But Noah never gave up. Once when he was "in the dumps a little," he wrote, "I wish to see you every day." He kept writing and visiting her, and the Greenleafs became fond of the famous author and patriot. He and Rebecca married and moved to Hartford in 1789. They had their first of eight children, Emily, in 1790.

October 1787

Oct. 26.	Ride to New York.
Oct. 27.	Lodge at Mrs Vandervoorts. dance on Long Island. Dine at Mr. Morton's.
Oct. 28.	Sunday. Dine at Mr. Watson's.
Oct. 29.	Breakfast with Mr. Davis. Pass evening at Mr. Loudon's.
Oct. 30.	Take tea at Dr Coggeswells.
Oct. 31.	Make a Contract with Mr. Saml Campbell for five years printing the Spelling Book.

FAMILY MAN

As the family grew, they often moved with Noah to his many workplaces. They didn't live with him in New York City where he edited two newspapers from 1793 to 1798. However, when Noah resigned, the family reunited in New Haven, Connecticut, and were rarely separated thereafter.

The Websters fit right into this busy port, site of Yale and home to many of Noah's friends. He soon became involved in local politics: he served on the city council, was justice of the peace, and later was elected to the state legislature.

Noah also contributed greatly to the education system of New Haven. He served on the school board and was eventually elected its president. He organized and supervised the building of a new school. And he was one of the founders of The Connecticut Academy of Arts and Sciences.

The Websters' large waterfront property (formerly that of infamous traitor Benedict Arnold) nurtured the family physically, intellectually, and spiritually. Orchards abounded—cherry, peach, apple, pear, and plum trees. Noah often coaxed his children to "eat your peck of fruit to-day." He used the estate as a natural-science classroom, teaching his children about plants, animals, and weather. He even darkened a pane of glass with smoke so that the family could look through it at an eclipse. Cupping a tulip, he told his daughter Eliza that "our heavenly Father made them all beautiful to make us happy." Noah entertained his children with his singing and flute playing. He also shared his love of words.

Over a fifty-year career, Noah tirelessly worked at many different jobs—often several at once.

BUSY NOAH

Noah taught at various levels, from common schools to colleges.

He practiced law in Hartford and New Haven.

He worked in New York City two different times, first in 1787 to edit and publish the *American Magazine* and again in 1793 to publish the city's first daily newspaper, *American Minerva*, and an internationally distributed weekly called the *Herald*. He later changed the names of the publications to the *Commercial Advertiser* and the *Spectator*, respectively.

As editor of the *Spectator*, he conducted the world's first medical study of an epidemic, yellow fever. After surveying hundreds of doctors, Noah linked the spread of disease with poor sanitation. He published his findings in the newspaper (and later in a book). Cities began building plumbing and drainage systems, and public health improved.

He was elected a councilman in Hartford, where he began the country's first insurance company, the Charitable Society, to serve the poor.

He helped found Amherst College in western Massachusetts.

He was a loving husband and beloved father of eight children.

Throughout it all, Noah continued writing educational books and essays about American unity. A textbook series, titled *Elements of Useful Knowledge*, included the first comprehensive American history and geography books, *Historical and Geographical Account of the United States* and *Historical and Geographical Account of . . . Europe, Asia and Africa* as well as a biology text, *A History of Animals.*

LEXICOGRAPHER

Noah's research for his book on yellow fever, *A Brief History of Epidemic Pestilential Diseases*, was one reason he became a lexicographer—a dictionary maker. "New circumstances, new modes of life, new laws, new ideas of various kinds give rise to new words." English dictionaries written by the scholar and author Dr. Samuel Johnson included neither scientific, medical, or legal words nor common words used, say, by merchants or the military. England's dictionaries certainly did not define words new to Americans, such as *skunk* and *chowder*.

Early dictionaries written by Americans were small and incomplete. One published in 1798 had only 4,100 words in 178 pages. Another in 1800 boasted over 25,700 words in 556 pages; but the same word was counted again for each of its different definitions. The word *shop* would have been entered as a verb meaning "to seek to buy"; it would have been counted again as a noun, as a place where people buy things. Plus, the dictionary still used many old British spellings. Noah studied the strengths and weaknesses of

As long as the written word has existed, since about 6000 BC, humans have tried to decipher what our symbols mean. Two inventions played important roles in the spread of the written word: paper, invented around AD 105 in China, and movable type, around 1430 in Europe. As more people learned to read words, the need for their definitions grew. Here are a few milestones in the history of the modern English language dictionaries:

1721	Nathan Bailey publishes the *Universal Etymological English Dictionary*.
1730	Bailey publishes the larger *Dictionarium Britannicum*.
1755	Dr. Samuel Johnson publishes his *Dictionary of the English Language*.
1798	Samuel Johnson, Jr., (no relation) publishes *A School Dictionary*, the first in America.
1800	Caleb Alexander publishes *The Columbian Dictionary of the English Language*.
1806	Noah Webster publishes *A Compendious Dictionary of the English Language*.
1828	Webster publishes *An American Dictionary of the English Language*.
1884–1928	Sir James Murray publishes *The Oxford English Dictionary* in ten volumes.
1961	Merriam-Webster publishes *Webster's Third New International Dictionary, Unabridged*.
1987	First Merriam-Webster electronic dictionaries.
1996	First Merriam-Webster Web site offering free access to its online dictionary and thesaurus.

these dictionaries. He vowed to make his bigger and better and, above all, more American.

Noah had always handled words as if they were precious silk threads. Now he would weave them into a luxurious blanket, tucking in everything American.

Beginning in 1800, Noah took six years to compile and define 40,600 separate words for *A Compendious Dictionary of the English Language*. The 408-page book sold for $1.50. Although Noah added many words, he chose *not* to include many vulgar words such as *turd* and *fart* that were in Johnson's book. He also got rid of English words that Americans didn't use anymore, like *jeggumbob*. And he made up a formal system of accent marks to show which syllable should be stressed. (He had included basic accents in his spellers.) The following year, Noah published a school dictionary, with 30,000 words in 312 pages. He charged $1.00.

LANGUAGE DETECTIVE

While putting the *Compendious* together, Noah already knew he wanted to build another, grander dictionary. In 1812, he wrote to a friend, "I am engaged in a work which gives me great pleasure; & the tracing of language through more than twenty dialects has opened a new & before unexplored field."

Noah would need a slower and less expensive lifestyle to continue his research. Later that year, he moved his family from New Haven to the farmland of Amherst, Massachusetts. Surprisingly, the boy who tried to avoid farm chores became a scientist of agriculture. He experimented with farming techniques, such as grafting fruit trees, applying different fertilizers, and conserving forests by thinning them. Almost every spring, he recorded the day he harvested his "first asparagus." He published his farming discoveries in the *Hampshire Gazette*.

Noah devoted plenty of time—about nine hours a day—for his language discoveries. He turned an upstairs room into a library, which he opened to area scholars and students. Writing at a semicircular desk, Noah surrounded himself with "friends": hundreds of reference books—dictionaries, encyclopedias, and grammar texts in many different languages. He taught himself eight more, including Arabic, Ethiopic, Danish, and Persian.

Still, his own library would not do. In 1822, Noah sold the house in Amherst and

moved his family back to New Haven— a residence smaller than their first home. He needed to be closer to grander libraries, such as Yale's. But his mission soon outgrew *all* American libraries.

Noah pioneered book promotion and mass marketing, beginning with his spellers and textbooks. He discovered that he could never shield himself totally from criticism. But he could reply to attacks with letters to the newspapers, explaining his ideas in more detail. He used the criticism as opportunities to gain publicity. Noah gave advance copies of his books to newspapers to review and to run excerpts. He publicized his donations of books, and he sponsored scholarships. His books were sold in several ways—at general stores, during his speaking events, and through the mail, sending sections by subscriptions. He sought endorsements from famous people such as Benjamin Franklin and George Washington and other influential leaders—university presidents, state representatives, and clergy. Praise for Noah's speller came from Colonel Timothy Pickering, a future cabinet member of Washington's, then later a Massachusetts senator: "The author is ingenious, and writes from his own experience as a schoolmaster, as well as the best authorities; and the time will come when no authority . . . will be superior to his own."

33

Noah needed to know *everything*! He traveled to England to research dictionaries written fifty to one hundred fifty years earlier. In Paris, France, at the Bibliothèque du Roi (King's Library), Noah found even older dictionaries and encyclopedias—and more of them. The one million bound books and eighty thousand manuscripts made him, for once, speechless.

"I cannot give you a description of my feelings," he wrote to his family.

The collection also included dictionaries covering science, natural history, and other subjects. He compared his own word tracings, or etymologies, with those of a three-volume French dictionary, and corrected his when needed.

"At no time for forty years past, have I been able to accomplish more business daily, that I have both in France & England," Noah wrote Becca on his sixty-sixth birthday in October 1824.

The following January, in Cambridge, England, Noah completed his seventy-thousand-word, *handwritten* masterpiece. "When I had come to the last word, I was seized with a trembling which made it somewhat difficult to hold my pen."

By the end of 1825, Noah had a contract with the publisher Sherman Converse of New York. Once Converse received special typefaces from Germany, the book then took eighteen months to print.

An American Dictionary of the English Language was finally published in November 1828, just after Noah turned seventy years old. Its 1,600 printed pages contained not only the definitions and pronunciations of seventy thousand words but also the histories of the words. The U.S. Congress—even scholars in England, France, and Germany—made the dictionary their official standard of English. Many ranked Noah as "the greatest lexicographer that has ever lived" and "the father of the American language."

But perhaps more important than his dictionaries was Noah Webster's contribution to education. His ideas, including free schooling, small class sizes, no hitting, books for each child—American history and literature books—earned him the nickname "Schoolmaster to America." Whether rich or poor, male or female, child or adult, all Americans, Noah said, had the right—and the duty as citizens—to learn.

"Unshackle your minds. . . . *Now* is the time and *this* is the country in which we may expect success in attempting changes favorable to language, science, and government. . . . Let us then seize the present moment."

AFTERWORD

If Noah Webster were alive today, he would be thrilled about the growth of the American language. Dictionaries now explain more words from world cultures, science, art, and technology (for instance, *taco*, *cyber*) and give new meanings for old words, such as *sneakers* and *laptop*. Noah would chuckle about how we have made up new words with the parts of old words, such as *automobile* from *auto* (Greek, meaning "self") and *mobile* (Latin, for "movable"). He'd dive right into creating acronyms like *SUV*, abbreviations such as *.com*, and words using both letters and numbers like *sk8*. Noah believed that languages are living things.

Noah's childhood home is still a living thing. The two-story house, now painted barn red, stands as a museum in West Hartford, Connecticut (then known as the west division of Hartford). There, visitors can see flax being woven, cast-iron pots and utensils hanging in the huge fireplace, and plain wooden furniture. They also can peer through glass at original dictionaries and Blue Backs, the great-grandfathers of the rich language-arts books we have today.

Two brothers, George and Charles Merriam, living in western Massachusetts, bought the copyright to Webster's dictionary in 1843. They, too, believed that languages are living things and brought out their first revision of Noah's dictionary in 1847. This was the first Merriam-Webster dictionary.

Today, lexicographers working at Merriam-Webster find new words (and new meanings for old words) by reading widely across all kinds of publications. Some editors scan computer manuals; others may peruse gardening magazines. Some days they read books for young children; other days they tackle college textbooks. They record their discoveries in a computer and on small cards that are filed in long narrow drawers. These words and meanings are then available for editors to consult when they create the next edition of the dictionary, a new mirror of our living language.

Noah believed that languages are living things.

CHRONOLOGY

1758   Noah Webster is born, October 16, in "west division," or West Hartford, Connecticut.

1772   At fourteen, Noah begins a two-year study of Greek and Latin with Reverend Nathan Perkins.

1773   The Boston Tea Party takes place to protest British taxes.

1774   In September, at age fifteen, Noah enters Yale College.

1775   Noah and Yale classmates boycott tea, build ramparts, and form a militia.

       In April "The shot heard round the world" at Lexington and Concord begins the American Revolution.

1776   On July 4 the Declaration of Independence is adopted.

1777   In September Noah joins his brothers and father's militia in a two-day march to halt an English fleet that is sailing up from New York City.

1778   In September Noah graduates from Yale College.

1779–1783   Noah spends the next few years teaching school, getting his law degree, practicing law, and writing essays.

1783   On September 3 the Treaty of Paris ends the American Revolution. In October Noah publishes his speller, Part I of *A Grammatical Institute of the English Language*.

1784   In January Noah begins diary.

       In March he publishes his grammar, Part II of *A Grammatical Institute of the English Language*.

1785   In February Noah publishes his reader, Part III of *A Grammatical Institute of the English Language*. In March he publishes *Sketches of American Policy*.

       Noah begins touring, lecturing, and selling his books—lifelong practices.

1786   Noah moves to Philadelphia in December to teach and participate in political discussions.

1787   From May to September the Constitutional Convention takes place in Philadelphia.

       In October Noah publishes his lecture/pamphlet *An Examination into the Leading Principles of the Constitution*. Noah tours, supporting ratification of the Constitution, which occurs in 1789.

       In October Noah moves to New York City to become editor of the *American Magazine*.

1789   In May Noah publishes *Dissertations on the English Language*.

       In October Noah marries Rebecca Greenleaf. They settle in Hartford, Connecticut, where Noah practices law and writes.

1790   In July Noah publishes *A Collection of Essays and Fugitiv Writings*.

On August 4 Noah's first child, Emily, is born.

1791 In October Noah publishes *The Prompter; or, A Commentary on Common Sayings and Subjects*.

1793 On February 5 Noah's second child, Frances Juliana, is born.

In August Noah is named editor of *American Minerva* and moves to New York.

Noah, an abolitionist, publishes "Effects of Slavery on Morals and Industry."

1794 Noah publishes *The Revolution in France*.

1797 On April 6 Noah's third child, Harriet, is born.

1798 The family moves to New Haven, Connecticut.

1799 On January 7 Noah's fourth child, Mary, is born.

In December Noah publishes *A Brief History of Epidemic and Pestilential Diseases*.

1800 Noah begins working on his first dictionary.

1801 On September 15 Noah's fifth child, William Greenleaf, is born.

1803 On December 21 Noah's sixth child, Eliza, is born.

1806 In February Noah publishes *A Compendious Dictionary of the English Language*.

On November 20 Noah's seventh child, Henry Bradford, is born and soon dies.

1808 On April 2 Noah's eighth child, Louisa, is born.

1812 In September the family moves to Amherst, Massachusetts.

1818–1821 Noah helps found Amherst College.

1822 During the summer the family moves back to New Haven, Connecticut.

1824 Noah begins research in libraries in France and England. He completes writing his masterpiece dictionary in January 1825.

1827 Noah revises the "Blue-Backed Speller" and issues *An Elementary Spelling Book*.

1828 Noah publishes *An American Dictionary of the English Language*.

1832 In August Noah publishes *The History of the United States*.

1833 In September Noah publishes an edition of the Bible.

1839 Noah publishes *A Manual of Useful Studies; for the Instruction of Young Persons of Both Sexes, in Families and Schools*.

1841 In March Noah publishes the second edition of *An American Dictionary of the English Language*.

1843 In May Noah publishes *A Collection of Essays and Fugitiv Writings on Moral, Historical, Political and Literary Subjects* and *A Collection of Papers on Political, Literary and Moral Subjects*.

On May 28 Noah dies in New Haven at the age of eighty-four. He is buried in the Grove Street Cemetery next to Yale University. Rebecca and the family lead a mile-long funeral procession of the entire Yale population and New Haven schoolchildren.

BIBLIOGRAPHY

All the quotations in this book are Noah Webster's own words and can be found in the following books listed under Primary Sources. If you can't visit the actual site of Noah's home, you can travel to www.noahwebsterhouse.org.

PRIMARY SOURCES

Dobbs, Christopher. Interviews by the author and tours of the Noah Webster House and West Hartford Historical Society, West Hartford, CT, April 2003–April 2006.

Morse, John. Interviews by the author, June 2004–April 2006. Tour of Merriam-Webster, Inc., Springfield, MA, September 2004.

Webster, Noah. *The Autobiographies of Noah Webster: From the Letters and Essays, Memoir, and Diary.* Edited by Richard M. Rollins. Columbia: University of South Carolina Press, 1989.

Webster, Noah. *Letters.* Edited by Harry R. Warfel. New York: Library Publishers, 1953.

Webster, Noah. *On Being American: Selected Writings, 1783–1828.* Edited by Homer D. Babbidge, Jr. New York: Frederick A. Praeger, 1967.

SECONDARY SOURCES

Babbidge, Homer D., Jr. "The Chief Glory of a Nation: Webster's Dictionary as an Act of Cultural Independence." Lecture, Sterling Memorial Library, Yale University, New Haven, CT, November 16, 1978.

Babbidge, Homer D., Jr. Editor's Notes and Introduction. In *On Being American: Selected Writings, 1783–1828,* by Noah Webster, p. 3–15. New York: Frederick A. Praeger, 1967.

Barlas, Pete. "His Perseverance Defined Success; Innovate: Webster's Love for American Language Made His Dictionary Tops." *Investor's Business Daily*, November 29, 2002, Section A, p. 3.

Bickford, Christopher P., ed. *Voices of the New Republic: Connecticut Towns, 1800–1832.* Vol. 1, *What They Said.* New Haven: Connecticut Academy of Arts and Sciences, 2003.

Cooney, Barbara, illus. *The American Speller: An Adaptation of Noah Webster's Blue-Backed Speller.* New York: Thomas Y. Crowell, 1960.

Ellis, Joseph J. *Founding Brothers: The Revolutionary Generation.* New York: Alfred A. Knopf, 2000.

Grant, Steve. "In a Word, I-N-D-E-P-E-N-D-E-N-C-E and Nobody Spelled It Like Noah Webster." *Hartford Courant,* June 10, 2001, p. H1.

Jones, Daniel P. "Digging Up Facts of Life: Students Learn About Noah Webster's 18th-Century Family." *Hartford Courant,* July 6, 2002, p. B2.

Jones, Daniel P. "Webster House to Build New Wing." *Hartford Courant,* October 18, 2002, p. B4.

Leavitt, Robert Keith. *Noah's Ark, New England Yankees, and the Endless Quest: A Short History of the Original Webster Dictionaries, with Particular Reference to Their First 100 Years as Publications of G. & C. Merriam Company.* Springfield, MA: G. & C. Merriam, 1947.

Merriam-Webster, Inc. *From Noah Webster to Merriam-Webster: The Evolution of America's First Dictionary; Celebrating 200 Years of American Dictionary Making.* Springfield, MA: Meriam-Webster, 2006.

Micklethwait, David. *Noah Webster and the American Dictionary.* Jefferson, NC: McFarland, 2000.

Monaghan, E. Jennifer. *A Common Heritage: Noah Webster's Blue-Back Speller.* Hamden, CT: Archon Books, 1983.

Moreau, Carolyn. "Paying Tribute with Words." *Hartford Courant.* March 29, 2004, p. B3.

Rollins, Richard M., Introduction. In *The Autobiographies of Noah Webster: From the Letters and Essays, Memoir, and Diary,* by Noah Webster, edited by Richard M. Rollins. Columbia: University of South Carolina Press, 1989.

Unger, Harlow Giles. *Noah Webster: The Life and Times of an American Patriot.* New York: John Wiley and Sons, 1998.

Warfel, Harry R. *Noah Webster: Schoolmaster to America.* New York: Octagon Books, 1966.

White, Timothy. "Will Artists Fight for Rights as Webster Did?" *Billboard Magazine,* May 20, 2000, p. 5.

FURTHER READING

Bailey, Carolyn Sherwin. "The Spelling Bee." *Child Life Magazine,* March 2001, p. 4.

Cooney, Barbara, illus. *The American Speller: An Adaptation of Noah Webster's Blue-Backed Speller.* New York: Thomas Y. Crowell, 1960.

Currie, Stephen. "In the Footsteps of Noah Webster: Making Their Own Dictionaries Clues Students to the Way Words Work." *Teaching PreK-8,* October 2000, p. 54.

Fritz, Jean. *Shh! We're Writing the Constitution.* Illustrated by Tomie dePaola. New York: Putnam, 1987.

Levy, Elizabeth. *If You Were There When They Signed the Constitution.* Illustrated by Richard Rosenblum. New York: Scholastic, 1987.

Melis, Luisanna Fodde. *Noah Webster and the First American Dictionary.* New York: PowerPlus Books, 2005.

Moore, Kay. *If You Lived at the Time of the American Revolution.* Illustrated by Daniel O'Leary. New York: Scholastic, 1997

Murphy, Jim. *A Young Patriot: The American Revolution as Experienced by One Boy.* New York: Clarion, 1996.

Rollins, Richard M. *The Long Journey of Noah Webster.* Philadelphia: University of Pennsylvania Press, 1980.

WEB SITES*

Cobblestone Publishing. www.cobblestonepub.com. See how to get the many back issues, articles, and teacher's guides about the eighteenth and nineteenth centuries, including issue 2004, vol. 10, "Colonial Philadelphia."

Merriam-Webster OnLine. www.merriam-webster.com. For teens and adults.

Merriam-Webster Word Central. www.wordcentral.com. Merriam-Webster's Web site for young children.

*Active at the time of publication

INDEX

Artist's Acknowledgments

For their invaluable assistance in researching the life and times of Noah Webster, thanks go to James N. Campbell of the New Haven Museum and Historical Society; Jennifer Matos and Christopher Dobbs of the Noah Webster House; Philip Zea and Anne Lanning of Historic Deerfield; Tevis Kimball and Kate Boyle of the Jones Library Special Collections; Fiona Russell of the Amherst Historical Society; and Lynn Stowe Tomb of Merriam-Webster.

For their time, knowledge, expert modeling, and comfort, thanks go to Liam, Aiden, and Conor Niles; Jair, Shea, and Will Cruikshank; Clare, Ava, Matthew, Michael S., and Michael J. Donelan; Mary Pickett; Devon and Dallas Elliot; Darcy McCurdy; Jince McCurdy; Pam Lawson and Larry Doe; Joan Brownstein and Peter Eaton; Carl Darrow; Beverly Staple; and Oliver Partridge and Samuel Gaylord.

For his patience, understanding, encouragement, and technical expertise, special thanks go to George Vachula. Without him this project could not have been completed. —M.V.

NOAH BY THE NUMBERS

NOAH WEBSTER'S DICTIONARIES

A Compendious Dictionary of the English Language	*An American Dictionary of the English Language*
Published in 1806	Published in 1828
6 years to write	20 years to write
40,600 entries	70,000 entries
408 pages	1,600 pages
Price: $1.50	Price: $20.00

MERRIAM-WEBSTER'S DICTIONARIES

An American Dictionary (Unabridged)	*Third New International Dictionary* (Unabridged)
Published in 1864	Published in 1961
4 years to write (team of 30 editors)	About 10 years (staff of about 70)
114,000 entries, 3,000 illustrations	450,000 entries
1,912 pages	2,726 pages

Ballad. n [Ir. moladh, W. moli praise, from mol, loud; probably from beul, beol, the mouth; like the Eng. bawl; but directly from or more probably from the It. ballata, a ball, a dance, a ballad, Gr. παλ w. to beat a frame; as ballads were originally songs, often accompanied with dancing. Hence Fr. balade, a song & baladin a dancer. In Pers. balantadan, is to praise. & balad - praised.

A song; originally a solemn song of praise; but the word is now used for a meaner kind of popular song.   Watts

Ballad. with utr dor. vint. To make or sing ballads.   Shak.
Ballader. n A writer of ballads.   Beesberry.
Ballad-singer n One whose employment is to sing ballads.

Either from Heb. & Ch. ◻ ┐ ┘ to weigh exactly, bring to a balance, or from
Ballast. n [Sax. bat, a boat. D. boot & D. last, load, burden, G. last = Ir. los lading, ballast; W. llwyth; Arm. lastr. ballast. & Bat. lost, boat lading continued changed into ballast. See boat. & Dan. ballast.

Heavy matter, as stone, sand or iron, laid on the bottoms of a ship or other vessel, to sink it in the water, to such a depth, as to enable it to carry a sufficient sail, without oversetting.
2 Figuratively, that which is used to make a thing steady.   Swift.

Ballast. vt. To place heavy substances at the bottoms of a ship or vessel, to keep it from oversetting.
2 To keep any thing steady, by counterbalancing its force.   Dryden.

Ballasted. pp Furnished with ballast; kept steady by a counterpoi force.

Ballasting. ppr. Furnishing with ballast; keeping steady.
Ballasting n Ballast; that which is used for ballast.   Shak.
Shingle-ballast, is ballast of coarse coarse gravel.

Ballatoon. n A heavy luggage boat employed on the rivers about the Caspian Sea.   Mar. Dict.

Ballet. n [Fr. ballet. It. baletto. See ball, a dance.] A kind of dance; an interlude; or dance in which some history is represented, or   Encyc.